DOGS

BOSTON TERRIERS

by Elizabeth Andrews

Cody Koala
An Imprint of Pop!
popbooksonline.com

Hello! My name is
Cody Koala

This book is filled with videos, puzzles, games, and more! Scan the QR codes* while you read, or visit the website below to make this book pop.

popbooksonline.com/boston-terrier

*Scanning QR codes requires a web-enabled smart device with a QR code reader app and a camera.

abdobooks.com

Published by Pop!, a division of ABDO, PO Box 398166, Minneapolis, Minnesota 55439. Copyright ©2023 by Abdo Consulting Group, Inc. International copyrights reserved in all countries. No part of this book may be reproduced in any form without written permission from the publisher. Cody Koala™ is a trademark and logo of Pop!.

Printed in the United States of America, North Mankato, Minnesota.

102022
012023

 THIS BOOK CONTAINS
RECYCLED MATERIALS

Cover Photo: Shutterstock Images
Interior Photos: Shutterstock Images
Editor: Grace Hansen
Series Designer: Colleen McLaren

Library of Congress Control Number: 2022941113

Publisher's Cataloging-in-Publication Data
Names: Andrews, Elizabeth, author.
Title: Boston terriers / by Elizabeth Andrews
Description: Minneapolis, Minnesota : Pop!, 2023 | Series: Dogs | Includes online resources and index.
Identifiers: ISBN 9781098243173 (lib. bdg.) | ISBN 9781098243876 (ebook)
Subjects: LCSH: Boston terrier--Juvenile literature. | Terriers--Juvenile literature. | Domestic Dog--Juvenile literature. | Zoology--Juvenile literature.
Classification: DDC 636.72--dc23

Table of Contents

Chapter 1

Proper Pup

Known as the American
Gentleman, the Boston
terrier has a smooth coat
that looks like a tuxedo. The
dog's chest is white. The rest
of the coat is black, brindle,
or seal.

Boston terriers were the first type of dog **bred** in the United States.

Watch a video here!

BLACK: solid patches with no undertone

BRINDLE: patches with streaks of brown and black

SEAL: almost brown in color with a reddish undertone in certain light

Boston terriers have a square head, short **muzzle**, and big round eyes. They are small dogs who weigh between 15 and 25 pounds (6.8–11.3kg). They have pointy ears and a **bobbed** tail.

Chapter 2

Personality

Boston terriers make good family pets because of their easy **temperament**. They are happy and playful dogs. They like going on short walks and playing with toys.

Boston terriers are the official state dog of Massachusetts.

Learn more here!

Boston terriers are easy to train. Training can start between two and five months of age. Boston terriers like to please. They make good **therapy dogs** and also do well in **agility** competitions.

Boston terriers' flat noses
can make their breathing
noisy. The dogs snort
and snore!

Their short **muzzles** also cause them to inhale extra air while eating. This can make them gassy.

Chapter 3

Pet Care

Boston terriers are sensitive to temperature. Owners need to keep homes cool during hot weather. The dogs might need boots or a coat to go outside in the winter.

Explore links here!

Boston terriers should get daily exercise through walks or play. These terriers can have breathing and teeth

problems as they get older.

They need a good vet to visit

for checkups.

Boston terriers need fresh, clean water and food. They also need a leash and collar with identification tags. A cozy crate or soft bed gives the pups a comfortable place to rest.

Two US presidents have had Boston terriers as pets. They were Gerald Ford and Warren G. Harding.

Chapter 4

Puppies

Like all dogs, Boston terrier puppies are born deaf and blind. They start hearing and seeing after ten to 14 days. Puppies can walk around three weeks old. At 12 weeks, they are ready for **adoption**!

Complete an activity here!

Making Connections

Text-to-Self

Would you train your Boston terrier for agility competitions? What tricks would you be most excited to teach?

Text-to-Text

Have you read about any other dog breeds? What did they have in common with the Boston terrier?

Text-to-World

Why do you think Boston terriers are so popular in the United States?

Glossary

adoption – the act of accepting an animal as a pet and taking on the responsibility of it.

agility – a sport where the dog is handled through an obstacle course.

bob – cut short.

bred – developed to act and look a specific way, or serve a certain purpose.

muzzle – the jaws and nose of an animal.

temperament – the manner of thinking, feeling, and acting that is normal for an animal.

therapy dog – a dog who goes with its owner to volunteer at places like schools, hospitals, and nursing homes, and is meant to bring comfort.

undertone – a slight appearance of a color.

Index

body, 7

care, 14, 16–17, 19

coat, 4, 6

ears, 7

eyes, 7

head, 7

health, 13, 16–17

muzzle, 7, 12–13

personality, 8, 11

play, 8, 16

puppies, 20

size, 7

tail, 7

training, 11

Online Resources

popbooksonline.com

Thanks for reading this Cody Koala book!

This book is filled with videos, puzzles, games, and more! Scan the QR codes* while you read, or visit the website below to make this book pop.

popbooksonline.com/boston-terrier

*Scanning QR codes requires a web-enabled smart device with a QR code reader app and a camera.